HISTORY OF COMPANY F, 1st REGIMENT, R. I. VOLUNTEERS

DURING THE SPRING AND SUMMER OF 1861

HISTORY OF COMPANY F, 1st REGIMENT, R. I. VOLUNTEERS
DURING THE SPRING AND SUMMER OF 1861

CHARLES H. CLARKE
A MEMBER OF THE COMPANY

WILDSIDE PRESS

HISTORY OF COMPANY F, 1st REGIMENT, R. I. VOLUNTEERS

Published by Wildside Press LLC.
<www.wildsidebooks.com>

INTRODUCTION

In the following pages I have endeavored to present a correct description of the service performed by Company F, 1st Regiment R. I. Volunteers, during the spring and summer of 1861. While many of my comrades who served in that company may differ with me in some of the statements I have made, still I think that all will agree that what I have presented is as correct an account as can be had at this late period of that service. Thirty years is a long time for men to remember the particulars of any event, unless some memoranda of the same is at hand. During that service I endeavored to keep as correct as possible a daily journal of events, and from that journal I have prepared this brief history of the company, and I trust that my comrades who may read this will excuse any inaccuracies that in their opinion may appear; for it is my desire to place before you a correct history of Company F, the first company of volunteers that left Newport on the 17th of April, 1861, for the defence of the Stars and Stripes in the great war of the rebellion.

CHARLES H. CLARKE.

CHAPTER I
CALL TO ARMS

Early in the month of April, 1861, several of the Southern States having withdrawn from the Union, forts, arsenals and navy yards within the limits of those States were taken possession of by the Confederate forces. On the 12th of April, Fort Sumter, at Charleston, S. C., was fired upon, and after two days' bombardment by the rebels, commanded by General Beauregard, the garrison, comprising seventy United States Regulars, commanded by Major Robert Anderson, surrendered the fort. Meanwhile the National Capital at Washington was in danger, and on the 15th of April Abraham Lincoln issued his proclamation, calling for seventy-five thousand troops for the defence of the city of Washington.

Governor Sprague, of Rhode Island, tendered the services of one regiment of Infantry, and one battery of Light Artillery, which being accepted by the Secretary of War, the Governor at once sent a telegram to Colonel George W. Tew, commanding the Newport Artillery company, asking how many men of his command would go to Washington for the defence of the Capital. Colonel Tew replied that he would go, with fifty men. April 16th, Colonel Tew received another telegram from the Governor, directing him to recruit his company to one hundred, and to report at Providence, armed and equipped, upon receipt of orders. At that time the Newport Artillery were as well equipped as any company in the State. They were armed with the latest improved Springfield rifles. They had just purchased, at their own expense, fifty artillery sabres of the latest French pattern. They had likewise, the year preceding, had made to their order new military overcoats, which no other company in the State was at that time provided with. These overcoats and sabres were afterwards purchased of them by the State of Rhode Island, and were used for equipping the 1st Battery.

On April 16th Colonel Tew called a meeting of the company, and after reading the telegrams received from the Governor that day, made a patriotic speech, and was followed by Mayor Cranston, who was present. Colonel Tew then requested those of the company that would volunteer to go to Washington, to step to the front, when thirty-three of the thirty-nine active members of the company responded. A call was then made for volunteers to fill up the company to the required number of one hundred men, and in a very short time there were more men applied than could be taken.

That evening the company paraded through the streets of the city, to the inspiring music of a fife and drum, and were dismissed at 10 P. M., to meet again on the receipt of orders from Providence, to be announced by the discharge of three guns on the Mall, and by the ringing of the church bells.

At 7 A. M., Wednesday, April 17th, a mounted courier arrived from Providence with orders for Colonel Tew to report that day in Providence with his company. Colonel Tew, upon the receipt of the order, sent word by return courier that he would be in Providence with his company at 2 P. M.

At 8 A. M., one of the company's brass guns was dragged by hand to the Mall and fired three times by the gun squad that had remained in the armory all night so as to be on hand when orders came.

Never before in the known history of the city was there so much excitement as was caused by the firing of those guns. Business of all kinds was suspended for the time being, and the people began to realize that the time had come for action.

When the orders came that morning, Colonel George W. Tew was at work at his trade, a mason, on Wellington Avenue. On receiving the order he laid down his trowel and other tools, adopted the trade of a soldier, and for four long years he served his country with credit to himself and to the State of Rhode Island.

First Sergeant A. P. Sherman was driving on his market wagon attending to his morning trade when he heard the signal guns. Leaving his team on the street, he started at once for the armory on Clarke street, and commenced to form the company.

In less than one hour the company were in line and ready to start. Like the minute men of Revolutionary times, they left their bench, their desks, and farm, at the call to arms. Thames street, Washington square and Clarke street were thronged with people. The artillery was at that time as at present the pride of Newport and it is not strange that so much interest was manifested, and, besides, they were about to leave home and friends, not knowing whether they would ever return. They went from pure patriotism and love of the Old Flag; and it is an undisputed fact to-day that had it not been for the promptitude with which the first troops responded to the call of the President, the city of Washington would have been taken by the rebel forces. At the armory there were there assembled many prominent citizens, Mayor W. H. Cranston and several of the clergy. Speech making and hand shaking were indulged in for some time, and at 11.30 A. M. the company marched to Sayer's Wharf by way of Clarke, Touro and Thames streets, escorted by about fifty past members of the company. On the wharf, Rev. Samuel Adlam, of the First Baptist Church, offered prayer, and was followed by Mayor Cranston and Hon. Charles C. Van Zandt, in brief addresses. Rev. Thatcher Thayer, who had for many years been chaplain of the Artillery company, and still holds that position, (1891) offered a touching prayer in behalf of the company and the cause for the support and defence of which they were now about to leave home, kindred and friends, after which the benediction was pronounced by Rev. Henry Jackson, D. D. A brief season was then allowed for individual leave-takings, and at 1 P. M. the company marched on board steamer Perry for Providence to form a part of Rhode Island's first regiment in the war of the rebellion.

Following is a correct roll of the company, as copied from the muster-out roll of the regiment:

COMPANY ROSTER

Captain,—George W. Tew.
1st Lieutenant,—William A. Steadman.
2d   "   Benjamin L. Slocum.
Ensign,—James H. Chappell.
1st Sergeant,—Augustus P. Sherman.
2d   "   Thomas S. Burdick.
3d   "   John S. Coggeshall.
4th   "   Edward S. Hammond.
1st Corporal,—John D. Washburne.
2d   "   Benedict F. Smith.
3d   "   Ray B. Tayer.
4th   "   Henry L. Nicolai.

PRIVATES

John A. Abbott.
Charles B. Barlow.
Albert N. Burdick.
George C. Almy.
John H. Bacheller.
Christopher E. Barker.

Charles Barker, Jr.
Andrew P. Bashford.
William Booth.
Daniel Boss.
Jeremiah Brown.
Adelbert P. Bryant.
Thomas Brownell.
Henry Bull, Jr.
Benjamin D. Carlisle.
Robert Carlisle.
Allen Caswell.
Charles H. Clarke.
Edward F. Clarke.
Frederic A. Clarke.
Gustavus A. Clarke.
Joshua P. Clarke.
David M. Coggeshall, Jr.
Lawton Coggeshall.
Robert D. Coggeshall.
Robert Crane.
Perry B. Dawley.
Benjamin F. Davis.
William P. Denman.
Lance DeJongh.
Silas D. DeBlois.
Stephen DeBlois.
William H. Durfee.
Henry T. Easton.
Benjamin Easton, Jr.
John F. Easton.
William J. Eldridge.
Edmund W. Fales.
John Fludder.
Augustus French.
Thomas J. Harrington.
Joseph J. Gould.
Rowland R. Hazard.
William Hamilton.
Samuel Hilton.
Benjamin C. Hubbard.
George A. Hudson.
Harris Keables.
William Keating.
Edwin A. Kelley.

Theodore W. King.
William H. King.
Israel F. Lake, Jr.
Thomas O. Lake.
Henry B. Landers.
John B. Landers.
Overton G. Langley.
Charles E. Lawton.
George P. Lawton.
Thomas H. Lawton.
David Little.
Charles L. Littlefield.
John B. Mason.
James Markham.
Daniel A. McCann.
William M. Minkler.
Walden H. Mason.
Michael A. Nolan.
George H. Palmer.
Frederic J. Peabody.
Edwin H. Peabody.
John P. Peckham.
Peyton H. Randolph.
John Rogers.
Benjamin H. Rogers.
John H. Robinson.
John F. Scott.
Thomas Scott.
Thomas Sharpe.
Bartlett L. Simmons.
John B. F. Smith.
George B. Smith.
Charles Southwick.
John Stark.
George W. Taber.
Edward Terrell.
William H. Thayer.
William Towle.
Arthur R. Tuell.
James P. Vose.
William H. Waldron.
George S. Ward.
Charles S. Weaver.
George R. White.

Edward Wilson.
William H. Young.

To be added to this roll, should be the names of James H. Taylor, John S. Engs, and James W. Lyon, members of the regimental non-commissioned staff, who were members of the company from Newport, but their names do not appear on the muster-out roll of the company.

On arriving at Providence, the company marched to Railroad Hall, on Exchange Place, where they were to be quartered until such time as the regiment could be uniformed and equipped. The organization of the regiment commenced at once. Ambrose E. Burnside was appointed colonel; Joseph S. Pitman, lieutenant colonel; John S. Slocum, 1st major; Joseph P. Balch, 2d major; Charles H. Merriman, adjutant; Rev. Augustus Woodbury, chaplain. All company officers were elected by the company, approved and commissioned by the Governor. The position in line of the companies and the letter by which they were to be known, was drawn by lot by the captains. The Newport company was designated by the letter F, and drew third position in line, which constituted them the color company of the regiment. In the making up of the non-commissioned staff, there were appointed James H. Taylor as hospital steward, James W. Lyon as ordnance sergeant, and John S. Engs as sergeant major; Edward S. Hammond was appointed as left general guide of the regiment.

As fast as the uniforms could be made, they were issued to the companies. These consisted of a light blue blouse, of the Garibaldi pattern, dark grey pants, and Kossuth hat, with the brim turned up on the right side, and fastened to the crown with a brass plate, eagle shaped. Instead of overcoats, we were provided with red woollen blankets, with a slit in the centre, to wear over our shoulders in bad weather; also one grey blanket, knapsack, to contain our extra clothing, haversack, canteen, tin plate, knife and fork, spoon, and tin cup.

CHAPTER II
OFF FOR THE FRONT

On Saturday, April 19th, the first detachment, made up of details from all the companies, to the number of nearly six hundred men, including the regimental band, of twenty-four men, were in readiness to start for Washington. The regiment formed on Exchange Place at noon, where they received a costly and beautiful regimental flag, of silk, presented by the ladies of Providence. Colonel Burnside, on receiving the precious gift, remarked as follows:—

"I know that the gallant men I carry away will prove themselves worthy of the beautiful banner presented to them by you. We are fully impressed with the fact that we take with us your most fervent prayers, and we shall constantly feel that your eyes are upon us. God grant that we may yet see the Union out of danger. Bidding you an affectionate farewell, and thanking you in behalf of my command, for your kindness, I feel that I can assure you in the name of each and every one of them, that no act of theirs shall ever cause you to regret this your generous and patriotic contribution to the cause we mutually cherish."

The flag was then given in charge of Company F, the color company of the regiment, Charles Becherer, of Company G, being detailed as color sergeant.

A short regimental parade was made through the streets of Providence to the wharf where steamer Empire State was lying with steam up, in readiness to take the regiment to New York. At about 2.30 P. M. the boat cast off her lines and steamed down the bay and through the harbor of Newport out to sea. When the steamer was passing Long Wharf, a salute was fired by a gun squad of the past members of the Newport Artillery. A salute was also fired from Fort Adams, as the steamer passed on her way out to sea.

Sunday morning, April 20th, arrived in New York. The regiment, with its baggage, was at once transferred to the United States Government transport Coatzacolcos, on board of which we remained all that day, and Monday steamed away for Annapolis.

A tug boat which spoke us in the afternoon, gave us the information that the Norfolk navy yard had been blown up and destroyed by orders from our government. At daylight the next morning we came in sight of Fortress Monroe, and sailing on up

Chesapeake Bay, anchored for the night, and the next day steamed up into the harbor of Annapolis and landed. We were kindly received by the officers of the United States Naval Academy, who furnished us with quarters in the government building for the night.

General Benjamin F. Butler, of Massachusetts, was there in command of the United States forces, composed mostly of New England troops.

Thursday morning we set out on the road to Annapolis Junction. We were told by inhabitants we met that we never would reach Washington, as the road was in the possession of Confederate troops and their friends; but we tramped along, and overtook the 71st New York Regiment at noon, halting an hour or two in their company, and after having had a good rest, about 4 o'clock resumed our march for the Junction, discovering no signs of the enemy as we proceeded, and at about 8 P. M. halted for the night. We encamped in a field beside the railroad, posting sentinels on all sides, as we expected an attack at this place. Camp fires were kindled, supper prepared and eaten, after which preparations were made for the night. The 71st New York coming up and halting at our bivouac, we exchanged greetings with them, furnished them with hot coffee, and informed them, as they took their departure on the road, that it was a short march for them to the Junction—"only nine more miles." A member of the 71st afterwards composed a song entitled "Nine Miles to the Junction," the words of which were as follows:

> *The troops of Rhode Island were posted along*
> *On the road from Annapolis station,*
> *As the 71st Regiment, one thousand strong,*
> *Went on in defence of the nation:*
> *We'd been marching all day, in the sun's scorching rays,*
> *With two biscuits a day as our rations,*
> *When we asked Governor Sprague to show us the way,*
> *And "How many miles to the Junction?"*
>
> *[Repeat:]*
>
> *The Rhode Island boys cheered us on out of sight,*
> *After giving the following injunction:*
> *"Just to keep up your courage—you'll get there to-night,*
> *For 'it's only nine miles to the Junction!'"*
> *They gave us hot coffee, a grasp of the hand,*
> *Which cheered and refreshed our exhaustion;*

We reached in six hours the long promised land,
For 't was "only nine miles to the Junction."

And now as we meet them in Washington's streets,
They always salute us with unction;
And still the old cry some one will repeat—
"It's only nine miles to the Junction!"
Three cheers for the warm hearted Rhode Island boys,
May each be true to his function;
And whene'er we meet, let us each other greet,
With "Only nine miles to the Junction."
Nine cheers for the flag under which we will fight,
If the traitors should dare to assail it.
One cheer for each mile that we made on that night,
When 't was "Only nine miles to the Junction."
With hearts thus united, our breasts to the foe—
Once more with delight will we hail it;
If duty should call us, still onward we'll go,
If even "nine miles to the Junction."

This was set to the air, "Tother side o' Jordan," and was adopted into the regiment, becoming one of our camp fire songs.

During the night, after the departure of the 71st, nothing transpired to disturb us.

At about 4 o'clock A. M. April 26th, we were once more on the road to the Junction, which we reached at about 5.30 A. M., and at once commenced loading baggage and provisions on the cars. At 9 A. M., everything being in readiness and the road reported clear, we started for Washington, where we arrived about noon, and were at once marched to the Patent Office, on 7th street, where we were to be quartered until a site for a camp could be selected.

Tuesday, April 30th, the second detachment of the regiment arrived, in command of Lieutenant Colonel Pitman, and on May 1st the regiment was paraded in front of the Patent Office, the occasion being the raising of the Stars and Stripes on that building. The flag was hoisted by President Lincoln, after which the regiment was drilled by Colonel Burnside, under review by the President and members of the Cabinet.

Thursday, May 2d, the Light Battery arrived from Providence, in command of Captain Charles H. Tompkins, and in the afternoon the entire regiment marched to the Capitol grounds, and was sworn into the United States service, by Major McDowell, of the Regular army.

CHAPTER III
LIFE IN CAMP

Preparations were at once made to go into camp. A detail of mechanics was made from the regiment, and under the direction of Lieutenant Walker, of Company E, the requisite buildings were erected, and on May 10th the regiment went into camp in their new quarters, on the Keating farm, near the Bladensburg road, about a mile north of the Capitol. It was named Camp Sprague, in honor of Rhode Island's Governor.

Ten rows of buildings had been constructed, parallel with each other, for company quarters, a row for each company, with a street about fifteen feet in width between the buildings. The quarters of each company comprised six squad rooms, each room having accommodations for a non-commissioned officer and eighteen men, and on three sides of each sleeping room were bunks; there was also an outer room, or porch, with a table extending lengthwise, for use as a dining room. The company officers occupied a building separated from the men by a narrow street. The regimental officers and band were very pleasantly located in a shady grove, in cottage shaped buildings, with piazza in front, standing in the rear of and at right angles with the company quarters.

We soon got settled in our new home at Camp Sprague, and commenced at once the duties of soldier life. Previous to this we had been in an unsettled condition, taking our meals at restaurants and using the Patent office for sleeping quarters, with not much duty to perform, except answering to roll-calls. Now, however, we knew just what was expected of us every day. Our duties commenced soon after daylight, ending at 9 P. M. At about 5 A. M. we were aroused from our slumbers by the beating of the reveille, which duty was performed by Drum Major Ben. West and his fife and drum band, when each man was required to turn out, take his place in line in the company street, and answer to his name. This duty was performed with a great deal of promptitude, at first, but after a while some of the boys did not get started out of their bunks in time to complete their toilet, and often would appear in line thinly clad, and it was no unusual thing to see some appear bareheaded and without shoes or stockings. One squad of the company was particularly noted for their tardiness at reveille. I don't think this was owing to any neglect on the part of the sergeant in charge; for Sergeant Hammond was wont to boast that he had "the banner squad," and he exacted of them everything in the line of duty. But two of his men appeared to be impressed with the notion that the nights in that latitude were too short to satisfy their demands for sleep. They would lie in bed and wait until the last roll of the drum, then tumbling out, they would have hardly sufficient time to take their places in line to answer to their names when called. One morning, during roll-call, the company were surprised to see running from the direction of Sergeant Hammond's quarters two men to all appearances of African descent. The First Sergeant, not knowing who they were, ordered them to stand aside, and then continued the calling of the roll. When the names of John B. M. and L. DeJ. were called, two "colored gentlemen" responded. The first sergeant, after roll-call, reprimanded them for appearing in such condition, advising them to in future be more prompt at roll-call. Some one or more merciless wags among their comrades had, during the silent watches of the night, and while they slept the sleep of the just, surreptitiously decorated their countenances with burnt cork. Of course Hammond knew nothing of it until their appearance at roll-call; but I do not think that afterwards there were any of Hammond's squad tardy at roll-call.

Directly after reveille came the sick-call, when those who required medical attention went to the hospital; breakfast at 7, guard-mount at 8 A. M., company drills and target practise from 9 to 11 A. M., dinner at noon. In the afternoon, battalion drill of the entire regiment, and at sunset dress parade, which on pleasant days was witnessed by a large number of the citizens and notables of Washington, including President Lincoln and members of the Cabinet. After the parade, the regiment formed in double column, closed en masse, when our chaplain, Rev. Augustus Woodbury, read a portion of scripture, followed by prayer, the service closing with singing the doxology by the entire regiment, accompanied by the band, with most solemn and impressive effect; tattoo roll-call at 9 P. M., taps at 9.30, when lights were extinguished and every man was supposed to be in his bunk for the night; but on many occasions there was more of supposition than reality. Notwithstanding the circumstance that we were United States soldiers, and as such bound to obey the army regulations, there were in nearly every squad men who would at times commit acts that had they realized the consequences if found out, they would not have suffered themselves to do. To take men from civil life, with no previous military training, and subject them to army discipline, is a difficult task to accomplish, and is a work of time; nor is it a matter for wonder that men forget their being soldiers and liable to severe punishment for misdemeanors.

After taps, it was the custom of the officer of the day to make the rounds of the camp to make sure that all lights were out and everything quiet in the company quarters. Sometimes this officer, if he manifested a disposition to be officious in the discharge of his duties, came to grief. There was one who, when detailed as officer of the day, generally had about all the business he cared to attend to, in the vicinity of Company F quarters, after taps. A candle would be left burning on the table in a room, to attract the officer's attention, who on seeing it would shout at the top of his voice, "Put out that light in Company F quarters!" Some one in bed would reply, "Go to H—ades, you old granny!" The officer, entering, would be deluged with a shower of tin pans and plates, placed on a shelf purposely rigged directly over the entrance, propped up by sticks, and at the proper time tripped by means of a string manipulated by some person to the officer unknown, the light being at the same instant extinguished by some one in the plot, the transaction overwhelming the officer with impotent wrath.

May 21st, John Abbott and Thomas H. Lawton were discharged from the company on account of disability, returning home.

May 23d, Governor Sprague left camp for home, to be inaugurated as Governor for another year. A detail of thirty men from the regiment was made to-day, and placed under command of Lieutenant Tower, of Company E, to operate a ferry for transporting troops across the river to Alexandria. They worked only nights, returning to camp at daylight in the morning. Company F furnished five men—Sergeant Burdick, John B. F. Smith, Andrew P. Bashford, George R. White, and Peyton Randolph, all of whom had been sailors previous to enlistment in the army, and consequently were familiar with that line of duty, and to them it was mere pastime.

Although away from home and friends, we as sons of old Newport could not permit 'Lection day to pass without notice. Nearly all of us had sent us from home boxes containing cake and blue eggs, and with these as a basis, we made preparations to celebrate the day. At sunrise we flung to the breeze a beautiful American flag, from the 1st sergeant's quarters. This flag, presented to us by Mr. William Vernon, of Newport, is still in the possession of the Newport Artillery company. A salute was fired by our battery, in honor of the day, and at 9 A. M. a table was spread in the quarters, with plenty of cake and egg pop. Private George C. Almy was deputed to call on and invite the company and regimental officers to visit us and partake of the good things. It was a very enjoyable occasion, Colonel Burnside and Chaplain Woodbury making some pleasant remarks.

May 31st, David Little, Fred J. Peabody and William Waldron, of Company F, were discharged on surgeon's certificate, for disability, and returned home.

About the first of June there were rumors in camp of a movement of troops; extra rations were cooked, and other preparations made for a forward movement.

June 6th, John S. Engs, who had been company clerk, was promoted to the position of sergeant-major of the regiment, to fill the vacancy caused by the resignation of John P. Shaw, who had been promoted to lieutenant in the 2d Rhode Island Regiment, and Augustus French was appointed company clerk.

CHAPTER IV
EXPEDITION TO HARPER'S FERRY

On Saturday, 8th of June, orders came for an expedition to Harper's Ferry. The day before starting, we had issued to us new caps of the French forage pattern, also white linen havelocks, to wear over them, which added greatly to the appearance of the men, being likewise a decided protection from the scorching rays of the June sun.

June 10th, the regiment broke camp, and marching to Washington took cars for Baltimore, arriving at which place we marched across the city to embark for Chambersburg, Pennsylvania. We had anticipated trouble in marching through the streets of Baltimore; but the roughs of the then rebellious city knew better than to oppose the passage of a regiment and battery armed and equipped as was the 1st Rhode Island. The regiment marched across the city from the depot where we landed, without a halt, with its band playing national airs. We were well supplied with ammunition, and the battery could have swept the streets of any mob essaying to obstruct its progress. We soon reached and boarded the cars, arriving at Chambersburg at noon, 11th, and starting again by rail for Greencastle, Pennsylvania, which place we reached at sunset the same day. After leaving the train we marched about three miles beyond the town, where we bivouacked for the night in a grove beside the road. We had no tents nor rations, the wagons not having come up. The regiment formed in a hollow square, stacked their muskets, and lay down on the ground, without covering, other than their blankets; sentinels were posted on the road, the battery parked in the rear of the regiment, and every precaution taken against surprise during the night. Tents arrived the next morning at daylight, but no rations. The tents we pitched and made preparations for a few days' stay. Troops were all the time coming and marching. The army to which we were at that time attached, comprised about nine thousand men, commanded by General Patterson, and was organizing for an attack upon Harper's Ferry.

June 12th, at noon, Governor Sprague rejoined us, having left Rhode Island at once on learning that we had departed from Washington.

At about sunset, while many of the regiment were seated on fences watching the passing troops, a Pennsylvania regiment came along the road, halting a few moments for rest in front of our camp. Directly some of our regiment discovered a man in one of the Pennsylvania companies who had been arrested by our regiment as a spy, while we were quartered at the Patent office in Washington. A rush was made for him, he was dragged from his company, and but for the intervention of some of our officers he would have been strung up on the spot.

Saturday morning, June 13th, we once more started, our destination being Williamsport, Maryland, distant fourteen miles. This was one of the hardest marches that we made. The weather was hot, the roads rough and dusty, and when we went into camp at Williamsport, there was only one officer and fourteen men of our company with the colors, present. The balance of the company were exhausted, and were straggling along the road, but by sunset they had all arrived in camp. We pitched our tents in the woods and rested the whole of Sunday.

Monday morning, June 15th, broke camp at daylight, and started on the road for Harper's Ferry. We had barely got started, when a mounted orderly arrived from Hagerstown, Maryland, with orders for Colonel Burnside to return with his regiment and battery to Washington, at once. Harper's Ferry had been evacuated by the rebels, who were also moving in the direction of Washington. Our regiment and battery set out at once on the road for Hagerstown, arriving there at noon. Without stopping we marched on through Funkstown, arriving at Boonsboro, Maryland, at 3 P. M., where we halted for a rest. We found the people of the place loyal, and disposed to show us every possible attention. We halted on the public square, or common, and the ladies of the town gathered in large numbers and supplied many of us with cake and other refreshments. Here the regiment and battery rested until 5 P. M., when the march was resumed. Entering a pass of the South Mountain, the acclivity looming up on both sides, every precaution was taken against any possible surprise by the enemy. The battery was divided, one-half in the [Pg advance and the remainder in the rear of the column.

At 9 P. M. we reached Middletown, where the people showed themselves in large numbers, as we passed their quiet homes. We made no stop at Middletown, but tramped along, tired and hungry, stopping about midnight and camping on a hill on the outskirts of Frederick City, Maryland, having marched thirty-six miles since daylight. Men from all the companies soon collected rails and built a camp-fire, illuminating the surrounding country and causing the ringing of a fire alarm in Frederick City.

At 4 A. M. June 18th, we broke camp and marched into Frederick, halting at some old barracks, said to have been built during the Revolutionary war. We were the first Union troops that had entered Frederick City since the commencement of hostilities, and the event naturally caused no little stir among the inhabitants of that semi-rebellious city. Nearly if not quite all its prominent citizens were in sympathy with the rebel cause, and we were consequently not regarded by them with any degree of favor. The presence, however, of twelve hundred well drilled and disciplined troops and a battery of six rifled guns, proved a quite potent reminder of what might be expected should there be any undue interference. Soon after entering Frederick, our company was marched to a restaurant and provided with an excellent breakfast, after which we returned to the old barracks. We were given permission by our officers to look about the city, with orders to report in camp at noon. Many of the citizens were found to be true Union men, by whom we were courteously received and kindly treated, and I don't believe that during our brief stay in town any member of the regiment, either by word or deed, left any unfavorable impression among the inhabitants. In the afternoon, just previous to the departure of the regiment, a deputation of Union citizens, both men and women, waited upon us and presented to Mrs. Kady Brownell an elegant American flag. Mrs. Brownell was the wife of Robert S. Brownell, of Company H, and when her husband enlisted, in Providence, she insisted on accompanying him, and was with the regiment during its entire term of service, in all its long marches sharing its privations and enduring its hardships. At the battle of Bull Run she was on the skirmish line with her husband, who was at the time a sergeant. She wore a uniform somewhat similar to that of the regiment, and was proficient in the use of a revolver and a short, straight sword, that she always wore suspended at her side.

At about 4 P. M., the regiment took up the line of march for the depot, to take cars for Washington. In marching through one of the principal streets leading to the depot, a crowd of rebel toughs issued from a side street, and following us, volunteered insulting remarks concerning us and the flag. Captain Tew, of our company, had at that time a colored servant, who had been with us for some time. This sooty individual, who was known by the name of John, had somewhere on the march picked up an antiquated sword and belt, which he had buckled on and felt very proud of. The sight of this negro, thus attired, appeared to kindle the wrath of Frederick City's chivalry to such an extent that they attempted to seize and make way with the boy, and for a short time the excitement ran high. The color sergeant, seeing that an attack upon us was threatened, drew his revolver and stood on the defensive. The right wing of the regiment, not being aware of the disturbance, continued on its march. Lieutenant Colonel Pitman, who was in command of the left wing, noticing the aspect of things, took prompt action, halting the companies, most of the men of F company loading their muskets, as they expected that the mob, which by this time had largely increased in numbers, would make an attack. At this juncture Colonel Burnside rode up and was about to issue some order to our officers, when a squad of city police, or home guard, appeared upon the scene and dispersed the mob, after which we resumed our march, soon arriving at the depot, where we took a train for Washington, reaching that place at daylight the next morning, June 19th.

Company F was immediately detailed to unload tents and other baggage from the cars. The regiment marched at once to our old quarters at Camp Sprague. While engaged on our work of unloading, our ever thoughtful commissary sent us a barrel of Camp Sprague ginger-bread, for lunch, and some good friend of the company, I never knew who, furnished us with a barrel of "conversation water" to wash it down with. We finished our work at 5 A. M., and marched out to camp, where we found a nice breakfast awaiting us. We resumed camp duties at once. Although we had been on a ten days' tramp, and had made one of the longest marches that had up to that time been made, in one day, by any troops, and had not during the whole time been over-stocked with rations, all the boys were in good condition and in readiness for any duty required of them.

Saturday June 22d, at 3 A. M., the camp was aroused by the beating of drums, and for a few minutes all was excitement, until it was announced that the occasion of the alarm was the arrival at our camp of the 2d Rhode Island regiment, via Washington, which place they had reached a few hours previous, and were waiting outside to allow us time to form our regiment so as to receive them in true military style, which was done a few minutes later, and K Company, Captain Charles W. Turner, our company asked to breakfast with us that morning. The 2d Regiment went into camp in tents in a shady grove adjoining us, and as long as we remained in Washington, both regiments mounted guard and had dress parade together every day. Many officers of the Second had seen service in our regiment previous to the formation of theirs, and we were intimately acquainted with many of its men, particularly those from Newport; and the men of our company will always look back with a great deal of pleasure to those days in the summer of '61, when the men of the two regiments passed so many pleasant hours in each others' society. The associations formed at that time, and later on in the war, between soldiers, were fraternal in their character, and to this day the same feeling exists among members of the Grand Army of the Republic, and will continue as long as the men that were associated with us shall live.

June 28th, the 1st and 2d Regiments, with the band of each, and the two Rhode Island light batteries, made a parade in the city of Washington, marching up through Pennsylvania Avenue to the White House, and counter-marching and passing in review before the President and other notables, among whom was the venerable General Winfield Scott, then so aged and feeble as to be unable to stand, sitting in a chair as the troops moved past. The parade was a grand showing for Little Rhody, over two thousand men in line, and so finely officered, armed and equipped. The Washington papers were enthusiastic in their praises of our soldierly appearance. In this parade we marched full company front, three ranks deep. The Hardee tactics were then in use in the army, but on this occasion we observed the three-rank formation prescribed in the Scott tactics previous to the war. The old General was highly pleased to see troops thus formed, as he was the originator of the three-rank formation, and I do not think he ever before or after saw so many troops arranged in that manner. We returned to camp at 5 P. M., and at evening parade Colonel Burnside complimented the troops highly for their soldierly bearing and general behaviour while in the city that day.

Soon after the arrival of the 2d Regiment, a change was made in the detail for camp guard. Previous to this there were ten men and a non-commissioned officer detailed every day from each company, for guard duty. But owing to the increased size of the camp, it was necessary that more men should be detailed, consequently an order was issued that a full company from each regiment be detailed every day for that duty. This new order of things was the occasion for considerable argument among the members of Company F, and we had men with us who were always ready for an argument, particularly if they believed they would be benefited by it. Albeit, while most of the company were ever ready and willing to obey every order emanating from proper authority, there were yet some who always reserved the right, as they thought, to growl. Some contended that it was contrary to army regulations, and that Company F could not be thus detailed, they were the color company of the regiment, and in case of an alarm, if the entire company were detailed for extraneous duty the colors would be without a guard. The matter was finally referred to Colonel Burnside, who at once decided that the color guard of eight men were exempt from general guard duty, but the balance of the company would mount guard. It would seem as though this should have settled the matter, but such was not the fact; in a few days Company F was detailed for guard duty, and at the proper time we were marched upon the parade ground, the customary evolutions pertaining to guard mount gone through with, and the order was given to march the guard off to the guard-house. Off we started, the band playing, but on our arrival at the guard-house our first sergeant was not with us, and on looking in the direction of the parade ground he was observed standing there alone, Robinson Crusoe like, "monarch of all he surveyed." On being requested by the adjutant to report for duty, he objected to doing so, and went to his quarters. He was soon ordered to report at headquarters, charged with disobedience of orders, but was allowed to give his reasons for not complying with orders relating to guard duty, which he readily did. They were that a 1st sergeant of a company was not a duty sergeant, and was consequently by the regulations exempt from such duty while in camp. The matter being referred to Colonel Burnside, that officer promptly ruled that the sergeant was right, and ever after the 1st sergeants of companies were relieved from service in that direction while in camp. It was a notable circumstance, which I wish to record here, that while Colonel Burnside always exacted of us a strict compliance with all orders, he was at the same time ready and willing to listen and act upon any complaint from officers or men, and invariably his decisions were just. He treated all alike, and was ever on the look out for the welfare and comfort of the men. As an illustration of General Burnside's ideas of duty, it was decided to erect a temporary structure for the purpose of holding religious services on the Sabbath. One day the sergeant-major made application to the captains of companies for a detail of mechanics for this work, in response to which details were sent from all except one of the companies, the captain of this company stating to the sergeant-major in response that he had no mechanics, his company being composed wholly of business men and clerks. This circumstance being duly reported to Colonel Burnside, he instructed the sergeant major to direct the captain of that company to detail ten men at once, as there were some foundation holes to dig, and he did not wish mechanics to do that sort of work.

Fourth of July was celebrated by both regiments in camp. There was a review of the regiments and batteries, and services held appropriate to the day, in which were included singing, music by the bands, and an oration by Rev. Father Quinn. In the afternoon we had sports of all kinds; a member of the second regiment gave a tight rope performance, and a member of the battery procured and turned loose a pig, well greased, said porker to become the property of the one that could catch and hold him; prizes were offered for the champion wrestler and clog dancer, respectively, both of which were captured by members of Company F, notwithstanding they had to compete with picked men from both regiments. James Markham took the clog dancer prize, and John H. Robinson laid every man on his back that presented himself before him.

We now commenced to have early morning drill. Every morning, directly after sick call, all the companies of the regiment moved out of camp in different directions, for one hour's drill before breakfast. This new order was not relished any better by the officers than the men, there was seldom more than one officer with us on these occasions, and often, as soon as a point outside the camp had been reached, the order to rest was given, particularly if there was a shady place handy; and I am of the opinion that those morning drills did not add much to our efficiency as soldiers.

On the morning of July 9th, the battery of the 2d Regiment were marching out for drill, and when a short distance from camp one of the ammunition chests exploded, killing one man, and mortally wounding the corporal of the gun, the latter dying in a few hours; the caisson was blown to pieces, and the wheel horses fatally injured. That afternoon funeral services were held in the camp of the 2d Regiment, and the remains of the deceased comrades were that evening put on board the cars for transportation to Providence.

About the 10th of July, there were rumors in camp of an intended advance into Virginia; extra rations were ordered, and new shoes issued to the company.

July 11th Edward Wilson, of F company, who had deserted at Frederick City, returned to camp, was placed in the guard house, and at dress parade, July 12th, his dishonorable discharge was read to the regiment. William H. Durfee and George S. Ward were the same day discharged on account of disability.

July 14th, we received orders to be in readiness to march at short notice, in light marching order, with no tents or unnecessary baggage. The order was received by the men, generally, with much enthusiasm, and as a decided relief from the monotonous existence incident to camp duty. The men had come out there to assist in putting down the rebellion and sustaining the honor of the flag, and as their term of service drew towards a close, they felt anxious that their journey to and sojourn in Washington and vicinity should be productive in results.

CHAPTER V
ADVANCE INTO VIRGINIA, AND BATTLE OF BULL RUN

On the morning of July 16th, came the order to move. F Company mounted guard, that morning, in marching order, with forty rounds of ammunition in our boxes, three days' rations in our haversacks, and blankets strapped on our backs. Both regiments formed on the parade ground at 10 A. M. Our company was relieved from guard and took its position in line, with the colors.

Both regiments marched into Washington, the battery of the 2d Regiment accompanying us. The camp was left in charge of about sixty men of the regiment, who had been on the sick roll, but had so far recovered as to be in condition for camp duty. Corporal Nicolai and Private Terrell, of our company, had been on the sick roll, but insisted on taking their place in the ranks, and marched into the city, but were obliged to return to camp the same night, not being sufficiently strong to endure the march.

Arrived in the city, we halted on Pennsylvania Avenue, waiting for the other regiments of our brigade, comprising, besides our own and the 2d, the 7th New York and 2d New Hampshire and 2d Rhode Island Light Battery, to join us, the whole comprising the Second Brigade, Second Division, commanded by General Hunter. It was late in the afternoon before we were ordered to move. All day troops had been crossing Long Bridge, and we had to wait until the whole of the First Division of infantry, artillery and cavalry had crossed. The army consisted of about forty-four thousand men, commanded by General McDowell; there was also attached to the column a battalion of United States Marines.

Our brigade crossed Long Bridge at about 4 P. M., and marched with our entire Division as far as Anandale, where we bivouacked for the night in the fields beside the road. Soon after halting, the boys began to think about supper, and little fires were kindled, coffee made, in our tin cups, and it is my opinion that the greater part of the three days' rations issued to us that morning were consumed that night. After supper, rolling our blankets about us, we lay down on the ground and enjoyed a good night's rest, notwithstanding that quite a shower of rain fell during the night.

We were on the road again soon after daylight the next morning. Hunter's Division, to which we were attached, marched on the direct road to Fairfax Court House. Soon after leaving Anandale, signs of the enemy's presence began to be visible: the roads were blocked with trees that had been felled and piled across the way, some of the obstructions so completely filling the road, that we were obliged to make a detour around them, through the fields. A company of sappers and miners attached to the 71st New York, and a detail of men from the 2d New Hampshire, with their axes cleared the road for the artillery to pass. Earthworks were occasionally found in the rear of these obstructions, thrown across the road; but in every instance they had been abandoned as we approached them; in some of these there were evidences of their having been occupied by the rebels the night previous.

The 2d Rhode Island, which was at the head of the column, was now ordered to send out skirmishers; also the carbineer company, Captain Goddard, of our regiment, was detailed for skirmish duty. We advanced cautiously, and soon a halt was ordered. Firing at the front was heard, where our skirmishers were driving the rebels back. Colonel Burnside, riding through our ranks, ordered us to load our muskets and be sure and obey all orders from our officers.

It was now about 9 A. M., and we knew that we were nearing Fairfax Court House, and knew also that the enemy were there in force and would resist our advance, which they no doubt would have done, had it not been that they had knowledge of the other two Divisions of our army under Generals Tyler and Heintzelman, who were advancing rapidly on other roads leading to Fairfax. After a halt of about fifteen minutes, the order to advance was given, and in a short time we marched into Fairfax Court House without having fired a gun, the rebels having retreated in such haste as to leave their tents standing, and in many of their camps we found clothing and baggage of various kinds. The 2d Rhode Island Regiment pursued the retreating enemy a short distance beyond the town. As we marched into the place the band played Yankee Doodle, and the color sergeant of the 2d New Hampshire mounted to the cupola and hoisted his flag.

We soon had possession of the town, and the regiments of the Division were stationed in different localities. We captured a Southern mail that had just arrived, and soon the ground in the vicinity of the Post Office was covered with mail matter of all kinds. We had quite a treat reading some of the letters that were picked up, particularly those written by fair rebels in the sunny south, who never dreamed that eyes other than those of their adored would scan their contents; but in time of war things are "mighty onsartin," to which love letters constitute no exception.

Nearly all the inhabitants had left the place on our approach, leaving behind their household furniture and goods. About all the residences of the so called chivalry were left in charge of one or more colored servants of the family, and in some instances these houses were protected from plunder through a guard placed over them by order of our commanding officer, while many of the homes of the poorer classes were broken into and plundered of articles of all kinds. For the first three hours of our occupation of the place, this state of [Pg affairs existed. The men, not being restrained of their liberty, roamed wherever they saw fit, and everybody, officers as well as men, appeared anxious to gobble up everything within their reach, (the term "stealing" in connection with it appeared to have become obsolete, there, articles looted being viewed in the light of spoils of war.) While some hunted for relics, others were in pursuit of something to eat, and others, still, would appropriate to themselves anything they could lift, or that "was not nailed down," whether it would be of any use to them or not, and I actually saw one man with more plunder than could be loaded into an ordinary express wagon. One man of our company who had looted a large linen table covering was so afraid that some one would steal it from him, that he made a square package of it and secreted it inside his blouse, which act of his, whether meritorious or otherwise, doubtless was the means of saving a life at Bull Run the next Sunday, when Allen Caswell was wounded in the stomach, the force of the shot being broken by the aforesaid table covering.

Soon after noon matters got quieted down a little. The entire army was at or near Fairfax; guards were posted on all the roads, and an order was issued that any man caught looting or committing any depredation should be committed to Alexandria jail for six months. But I am of the opinion that if the guards had seen one-half the stealing, or heard the dying squeals of those orphan pigs as they were being slain for supper that night, Alexandria's jail would have been a full house, and the fighting force of the army materially reduced. All the companies of the regiment had one or more men that excelled others not only in their proficiency as soldiers, but they were "professors" in any art or device that tended to add comfort and enjoyment to themselves, particularly when in an enemy's country, and under the necessity of providing their own rations. Just such a man as this we had in our company. James Markham never was known to have an empty haversack, and always managed to procure a full supply of rations, even at times at great personal risk. Just before dark on the afternoon of the day of our occupation of Fairfax, and after the before mentioned order had been given, this man Markham was on guard on a narrow road leading out of the town; on the side of the road where he was pacing was a tight board fence, and on the side opposite a zig-zag, or "Virginia" rail fence. Markham's attention was called by some one to a shoat pig that had all day escaped the "slaughter of the innocents," and was at that moment making the best of his way toward the maternal nest. The temptation on Markham's part to capture this sprig of porkdom was too mighty to be overcome by any lingering fear of Alexandria's dungeon, so instantly clapping his musket to his shoulder he blazed away, with the result of piggy's dropping in his tracks, without so much as an audible grunt. He sprang out, and had barely secured his prey, when a mounted officer with a squad of cavalry came galloping down the road. Markham proved himself equal to the occasion; quick as thought he tucked the hind legs of the animal underneath his waist-belt behind him, and backing up against the fence, coolly presented arms to the provost guard as they approached, and in reply to the officer's inquiry, "Who fired that shot?" answered, "It was a sentry beyond, down the road." The guard rode on, down the road, but it is presumed they never learned with any degree of accuracy "who fired that shot."

Our company was detailed for picket guard, that night. Brigade guard mount took place in the woods at sunset. Our regimental Band, led by the veteran Joe Greene, played his familiar piece, "The Mocking Bird." Our company was marched in the direction of Leesburg, and posted in the edge of the woods, where picket guard head quarters were established. At about 11 P. M., about one-half of our company relieved a company of the 14th Brooklyn, the balance of the company not going on until 1 A. M. There was occasional firing by the outer picket, or cavalry vidette, during the night. General McDowell had his headquarters that night in a covered carriage in the rear of an old blacksmith shop, privates Charles E. Lawton and Silas D. DeBlois, of F Company, being on post near the carriage.

At daylight, July 18th, we were ordered to report to the regiment. The army now started on the road to Centreville, and marched until about 9 A. M., when a halt was ordered. We lay in the road until about 2 P. M., waiting for the divisions on the other roads to come up. At about 3 P. M., firing was heard in the vicinity of Centreville, and we started at once, for some distance going on the double-quick. The occasion of the firing was soon ascertained to be that some of the troops of the First Division having advanced to the vicinity of Blackburn's Ford, were fired upon by the enemy, who were there in force, and after an engagement of about an hour the Union troops fell back, having lost about twenty men. We continued on our march that afternoon, to near Centreville, where we were ordered to camp. Hunter's entire division were encamped in the fields on both sides of the Warrenton Road, and we were that night given to understand that we would probably remain there a day or two; consequently the next morning, July 19th, we commenced to construct temporary huts of pine trees and boughs for a shelter. That afternoon we had fresh beef sent us in the shape of live cattle, which were distributed to the troops, two to each regiment. Sergeant Major John S. Engs, of our company, asked the privilege of shooting one of these animals, which being granted, he armed himself with a Burnside carbine and fired at about twenty paces, striking the ox in the fore shoulder; the animal started on the run, everybody after him, the sergeant major leading the charge. The ox, after a chase of half an hour or more, succumbed to exhaustion and was readily despatched; the remaining ox was killed by a man who understood the business. We broiled, fried and stewed our fresh beef that night, and made ourselves as comfortable as possible.

Saturday, July 20th, we loafed around camp, wrote letters home, and visited other camps. At sunset we had dress parade, when orders were read to be in readiness to march at a moment's notice, and for no man to leave his company during the night. Our dress parade was witnessed by General McDowell, his staff and officers, besides officers and men from other regiments; both the Rhode Island regiments were in line. After dress parade the usual religious services, (which were never omitted while in camp,) were held, followed by the singing of the Doxology. To many who stood at parade rest, that evening, listening, with heads uncovered, to those words of comfort and encouragement from our chaplain, it was to be the last attended on earth, for ere the setting of another sun, they would be lying dead on the fields of Manassas. At tattoo roll-call we were informed by our officers that our regiment would probably march at daylight. The boys rolled their blankets around them, and lying down, secured what little sleep they could, with thoughts busy with the dear ones at home and the probable events of the morrow.

At about 2 A. M. Sunday, 21st, the call sounded, and on every side and in all directions was heard the sound of the bugle and the drum, calling the soldiers from their sleep; and before the echoes of those bugle notes had ceased reverberating among the Virginia hills, our brigade was in line on the road, and ready to move. We were fully assured in our minds that a battle was to be fought that day; in fact Colonel Burnside had the day before stated to our officers that, although the period for which we enlisted had expired, he did not purpose to turn back at such a time, in the face of the enemy, and when the government needed our services; and it is to the credit of the regiment, and the State of Rhode Island, that regardless of the expiration of our term of enlistment we manfully did our duty during that campaign.

The order to march having been given, we tramped steadily along the Warrenton Road, no sounds being heard save the steady tread of the soldiers, and the occasional low words of command from the officers; the stars were still visible, and the nearly full moon was going down behind the western hills. At about daylight we passed through Centreville, and soon arrived at the small bridge at Cub Run. While on the road that morning, we were quite surprised to see Theodore W. King, of our company, join us. He had been quite sick in the hospital at Centreville for two days, but hearing of our regiment passing on the road, he left the hospital and started for his company, saying that if there was any fighting to be done, his place was with Company F. King, though only a mere boy, did his duty manfully on that eventful day, and about noon, in the heat of the battle, fell, mortally wounded.

Just before arriving at Cub Run, we met on the road a regiment and light battery going to the rear. In reply to questions, they said their time was out, and they were going home. This regiment, the 4th Pennsylvania, and the battery of the 8th New York, were the recipients of comments from our men not in the highest degree complimentary to them as men and soldiers, turning back in the face of the enemy, and that must have caused their cheeks to tingle with shame.

The whole three divisions of the army were now in the vicinity of Cub Run. The first division, General Tyler's, was ordered to cross, after doing which these troops advanced along the road to near the Stone Bridge. We crossed Cub Run bridge at 5.30 A. M., after which we struck off to the right through the woods from the main road.

At precisely 6 A. M. the first gun was fired, by Tyler's forces, the object being to engage the enemy's attention while the second division could get into position on the left and rear of their lines. Soon after entering these woods, K and F Companies of the 2d Rhode Island, and the carbineer company of our regiment, were thrown out as skirmishers. When we entered these woods we had with us a guide, dressed in citizen's clothes, riding a grey horse at the head of the brigade, but after firing began he disappeared from view.

At 10 A. M. we arrived at Sudley Ford, where we were to cross. General McDowell and staff met us, and we were informed by them that the enemy were moving a large force to meet us. After a short halt for the purpose of filling our canteens, we forded the stream. The firing of Tyler's troops could now be distinctly heard. We marched on up the road, past Sudley Church and a number of farm houses; a female standing at the gate of one of these latter made the remark in our hearing that they were all ready for us, and that she hoped we would all be killed before night.

Soon after passing these houses, the 2d Rhode Island, who were in the advance, continued on in the main road, our regiment branching off into and through a cornfield. Our skirmishers were now engaged with those of the enemy, and driving them back; shells were exploding around and above us as we again came out upon the road. Soon we passed a soldier lying near a fence, wounded. It proved to be William McCann, of K Company, (of Newport) of the 2d Rhode Island; he had been struck in the head by a fragment of shell, and died soon after. I think he was the first man wounded belonging to our brigade.

Our entire brigade was now halted in a huckleberry pasture, on the edge of some woods. In front of us was a rising ground, of which the enemy apparently had gained possession. Shot and shell were falling among us on every side. The Second Rhode Island, with their battery, were at once ordered to advance toward this rising ground, or hill, and in doing so the enemy opened on them, and for about twenty minutes we stood watching them, with no orders to advance to the assistance of our sister regiment. At this time the division commander, General Hunter, had been wounded, and Colonel Burnside being the senior Brigadier, took command of the entire division. He at once ordered the 71st New York to the assistance of the 2d Rhode Island. They advanced a short distance, and then lying down, refused to proceed further, until their two howitzers, which one of their companies were dragging by means of ropes, arrived to their support. Colonel Burnside then gave the command for the 1st Rhode Island to advance. Before moving, we received orders to unsling blankets and haversacks and lay them on the ground at our feet. We marched away and left them, and never saw them again. We came up in line of battle on the right of the 2d Regiment and at once commenced firing. Soon the men of F Company that were detailed to serve in the carbineer company joined us; they had been on the skirmish line all the forenoon, but became somewhat mixed when the firing commenced, and were ordered to report to their respective companies. John Rogers was one of the detail, and he was wounded in the leg while running across the field to join us.

Our regiment was so posted, that to preserve the line it was necessary to divide our company by a rail fence, a portion on each side. John P. Peckham was shot in the head and instantly killed, and when he fell, his musket which he was using fell over the fence. Our color sergeant, Charles Becherer, was shot in the right shoulder and disabled. Albert N. Burdick, 1st color corporal, then took the flag, and was soon wounded in the arm by a musket ball. At this time Governor Sprague, who was acting as aide for Colonel Burnside, rode through the line to go to the left, when his horse was struck by a rifle ball and fell dead, the Governor going down with him. Captain Tew and Sergeant Sherman went to his assistance, helping him to regain his feet; he was considerably bruised, but not otherwise injured. After two color bearers had been wounded, the regimental flag was taken and held by Private Robert D. Coggeshall, until, by order of Captain Tew, he was relieved by Private William Hamilton, of the color guard.

Shot and shell were flying in all directions; we had lost a number of men, and the other companies of the regiment had suffered considerable loss. An officer now rode in front of our regiment and gave the order to cease firing, as we were shooting our own troops. The smoke, which had occasioned this, soon lifted in our front, when we discovered a regiment bearing the union flag marching up the hill in our direction. When a short distance from us, they gave us a volley, which we returned at once, when they turned and retreated down the hill. This regiment was the 4th Alabama, and their colonel, Egbert Jones, was carried to our field hospital, mortally wounded. With others of our regiment I went over the field after the firing had ceased, and our conclusion was that they were amply repaid for the cruel and unmanly deception practiced upon us. It was never known who the officer was that gave the order to cease firing; he appeared in front of our lines, mounted, with sword uplifted when he gave the order, which was recognized by our company officers, they mistaking him for an aide-de-camp or staff officer. It was, however, the opinion of many of the regiment at the time that he was a rebel officer.

Soon the firing in our front ceased. Our ammunition was all expended, we having been under fire for nearly four hours, and had driven the enemy from that portion of the field. This position, from which we had forced the enemy to retire, and which we then held, is known as Buck's Hill, and was regarded as a position of much importance for our forces.

The Third Division had now arrived, and were coming up to our support, and a battalion each of Regular [Pg infantry and United States Marines now came up and occupied our position, while our brigade was marched back into the woods for a brief rest and for a fresh supply of ammunition. Having stacked our muskets, the roll was called by the 1st sergeant, and men detailed to look after the dead and wounded. George C. Almy, Christopher Barker and myself were detailed to go for water. Taking as many of the men's canteens as we could carry, we wended our way toward a small, one-story gambrel roof farm house, which was being used by our surgeons as a field hospital, near which was a well of water. The grounds about the house were covered with wounded and dying men, and it was almost like fighting, to get a supply of water from that well. We however succeeded in filling a portion of our canteens and returned with them to the company. Almost immediately after our arrival back to where the company were resting, the order was given to "fall in." Heavy firing was now again heard on our right, and our officers informed us that the regiment was to change position. Soon troops began to march past us in great confusion; our regiment marched out upon the road and halted. A body of troops passed us headed for the rear, among them two companies of Regular cavalry, whose principal participation in the day's engagement had been the performance of semi-aide-de-camp duty.

We were by this time satisfied in our minds that our army was retreating. At this juncture our brigade started back on the road along the edge of the woods, and soon reached the Warrenton road leading to the Stone Bridge. Our regiment preserved good order until they had nearly reached the bridge; the enemy had a battery in position to rake the road over which the retreat was being conducted, and on arriving in proximity to the bridge, we found it to be completely blocked with teams; a large army wagon had, in crossing, been struck by a shell and the horses killed. The battery of the 2d Rhode Island Regiment were there, and four of their six guns; after getting one of these over, they dismounted and spiked the remaining three, the men and horses fording the stream. In our regiment it was impossible to preserve order, and ours, like that of the others, became a go-as-you-please march in fording the stream; Governor Sprague strove to halt the regiment and make a stand to beat back the enemy, whereupon Colonel Burnside very promptly informed the Governor, in unmistakable and incontrovertible language, that himself was in command of the 1st Rhode Island Regiment. After crossing, the road branched off to the left, beyond the range of the enemy's fire, and our regiment re-formed and waited until most of the demoralized troops had passed, after which we marched in good order back to our bush camp at Centreville that we had left in the morning, reaching there at 9 P. M., tired, hungry, thirsty and dusty, and many of the regiment wounded. To add to our general discomfort, a drizzling rain had set in, and we were without blankets, having, as before stated, left them on the field, with our haversacks, before going into action. We, however, lay down in our bush huts, expecting to remain until morning; but about midnight we were aroused and ordered to start on the road to Washington. The drizzle had not abated and the night was dark; we had been in a state of continued and unusual activity since 2 o'clock the previous morning, and in addition had been all day without food. Footsore and weary we started on our march of twenty-six miles to Washington, and soon after daylight, Monday, July 22d, reached Long Bridge, where we made a halt and rations were served to us, and at 8 A. M. we crossed over to Washington, and marched across the city to our old home at Camp Sprague. The roll was called, a ration of whiskey was given us, and all turned in for a much needed and well earned rest.

OPINIONS ON THE BATTLE

Many opinions have been given as to the causes that led to the defeat of the Union army at Bull Run. General Sherman, who commanded a brigade in the battle, said it was the best planned and worst fought battle of the war. It has been said by some writers that the plans of the commanding general were not carried out, and that each of the three division commanders whose forces were actually engaged acted on their own responsibility and were governed by circumstances. It is a fact well known to-day, that the Union army, at or in the vicinity of the battle field, were in numbers quite sufficient to have at least held any and every position that a portion of the army had gained. On a map now in possession of Charles E. Lawton Post, G. A. R. of this city, of Bull Run battlefield, drawn under the direction of Generals McDowell and Beauregard, by order of the War Department, the position of every regiment and brigade of both armies at the commencement of the engagement is defined, and in a note appended to the map it is stated that the engagement was commenced by the Burnside brigade, and it is a historical fact recognized at this time, that the battle was fought and won by the Second Division, commanded by Burnside, General Hunter having been wounded before the troops had been brought into position, supported by no other troops, until noon, when a brigade of the Third Division, which had followed us through the forest road, came to our assistance. From 9.30 A. M. to 1 P. M., these seventeen regiments of infantry and four light batteries, unaided by any other troops, fought and drove the enemy from their position on Buck's Hill; and when the two brigades of Tyler's First Division, commanded by Generals Sherman and Schenck, crossed Bull Run river, over Stone Bridge, at 1.30 P. M., there was not a rebel force of any description on the north side of Warrenton road, west of Stone Bridge. At this time victory was assured for the Union army. At the Stone Bridge was Tyler's entire division, comprising fifteen regiments of infantry and three batteries, the Fourth Division, General Runyon, with seven regiments, Fifth Division, General Miles, eight regiments, and one battery. Of these thirteen thousand men, only two brigades of the First Division crossed the river in the afternoon, and they were engaged only about one hour, namely, in the vicinity of the Henry House, when they were repulsed by the enemy, whose forces were now all concentrated at that point. Rickett's Regular battery (formerly Magruder's stationed at Fort Adams previous to the war) was lost, recaptured, and lost again. These two brigades of the First Division retreated, panic stricken, and our reserve of twelve thousand men, at Stone Bridge, retreated without firing a shot, while our Division, the 2d, was holding the position we had gained in the morning. This was the supreme moment, when a Sheridan or a Warren would have swept the opposing forces from the field, or captured their entire army. Colonel Burnside, seeing the aspect matters had assumed, formed his troops into line and fell back to the Warrenton road, fearing he might be cut off at Stone Bridge. Hunter's Division covered the retreat and were the last troops that crossed the bridge, and was the only Division of the army that occupied its former quarters, as these did, at Centreville that night.

DAY AFTER THE BATTLE.

The day after the battle was a busy one in camp; men were straggling in all day, some of them that we had left among the wounded at the field hospital on our departure the evening previous, who had managed to hobble along on the road, and after a while reached camp. Some of these, owing to the darkness of the night, had taken the wrong road from Fairfax and brought up at Alexandria, whence they set out anew, reaching Long Bridge and the camp some hours later. Among these latter was John Fludder, who did not arrive until Monday afternoon, when he surprised us by bringing with him the regimental flag, which we had supposed to have been lost when the regiment "straggled" at Stone Bridge, as no one could give any information in regard to it. Fludder found it where it had been dropped in the confusion of retreat, and in order to save it tore it from the staff and secreting it about his person, thus brought it in. Samuel Hilton, who had been left on the field for dead, also came straggling in; he had been hit in the temple by a partially spent fragment of a shell and laid out senseless and inanimate, and was afterwards revived by the drizzling rain, as were also quite a number belonging to other regiments.

Company F had its full share of losses in killed and wounded. The first man of the company wounded was John B. Landers, shot through the wrist; then followed John Rogers, shot in the leg, Charles Becherer, color sergeant, wounded in the shoulder, Albert N. Burdick, color corporal, wounded in the arm, John P. Peckham, shot in the head and killed, Andrew P. Bashford, shot in the breast and taken prisoner, Theodore W. King, shot through the groin, mortally wounded, taken prisoner, and afterwards died in Philadelphia, when on his way home, Thomas J. Harrington, shot in the head and killed, Allen Caswell, shot in the stomach, Henry T. Easton, wounded in the arm, Samuel Hilton, wounded as above stated, Bartlett L. Simmons, taken prisoner, Robert Crane, never accounted for, but supposed to have been killed during the retreat.

July 24th, Doctor David King and Alderman James C. Powell, of Newport, arrived in camp. Doctor King obtained a pass through the lines for the purpose of attending his son, wounded as above stated, and who was a prisoner in Richmond. Alderman Powell was deputed by the city government of Newport to look after the sick and wounded of Company F on their way home.

Orders were received, July 24th, to make preparations for return to Rhode Island, as our term of service had expired. Colonel Burnside offered the services of the regiment for a longer time, as it was expected that the rebels would make an attack on Washington; but it was thought our services would not be needed, and preparations for departure were accordingly made. On Thursday, July 25th, we had dress parade for the last time in Washington. After the parade, the 2d Regiment was formed in line directly opposite and facing us, and the men of the two regiments exchanged muskets, each with the man opposite him; the muskets of the Second were old, smooth bore, altered over, while those of the First were the latest improved Springfield rifles. During the evening, we improved the opportunity to visit the camp of the Second, bidding them good bye, and receiving such messages and tokens as they desired to send home to friends.

CHAPTER VI
"HOME, SWEET HOME."—ARRIVAL. —FLAG PRESENTATION

At 9 P. M., 25th, the command was given to "Fall in;" the line was formed, we marched into the city, and at midnight bid farewell to Washington, the cars taking us into Baltimore at daylight, where we waited on the streets all the forenoon for the special train that was to take us to Philadelphia. We got away from Baltimore at 2 P. M., arriving in Philadelphia in the evening. We had been expected, and were entertained by the citizens with a fine collation at the New England rooms.

We left that city at 2 A. M., July 27th, arriving in New York soon after daylight, where the regiment embarked on board steamers Bay State and State of Maine, for Providence. Each steamer took five companies, ours being on the State of Maine, on board of which we were given a nice breakfast. We steamed out of New York at about 11 A. M., July 27th, the transports proceeding slowly to avoid arriving in Providence at a late hour in the day. At 10.30 P. M. we were off Beaver Tail light; F Company was called and formed on the hurricane deck, Captain Tew arranging with the steamer captain to sail through the inner harbor of Newport. When opposite Fort Greene, a squad of the Newport Artillery fired a salute, which was answered with cheering by F Company, and the blowing of the steamer's whistle. Both steamers proceeded up the bay and anchored, it being the wish to not land before daylight.

At 6 A. M. Sunday, July 28th, landed, and, escorted by the militia of the state, marched through the city to Railroad Hall, Exchange Place, where a substantial breakfast awaited us. After breakfast and speeches by Bishop Clark and others, the regimental companies residing outside of Providence were ordered to their homes, to report again in Providence August 2d.

F Company, escorted by the past members of the Newport Artillery, Colonel Fludder in command, and the Old Guard, both of which companies had that morning come from Providence to receive us, left for Newport on steamer Perry at 11 A. M., arriving at Sayer's Wharf in Newport, at 1 P. M.

On our arrival we found the wharf and streets of the city through which we were to pass crowded with people of all ages and both sexes, as though the whole of Newport had turned out to greet us. Services were omitted by the churches, all evidently regarding it as a duty appropriate to the Sabbath to welcome to their homes those who had gone forth to peril their lives at their country's call. Tears dropped from many eyes, as those were remembered who had left home with us, but would never return.

We marched up Thames street, our sick and wounded in carriages, through Touro street and Bellevue Avenue, to Touro Park, where we were welcomed in addresses by Mayor Cranston and other city officials. On invitation of Mr. William Newton, proprietor of the Atlantic house, we partook of an excellent dinner at that hostelry, after which a short street parade was made to the armory on Clarke street, where we were dismissed, with orders to report again on the 2d of August.

On Friday, August 2d, we reported at the armory and proceeded to Providence; we received our pay and were mustered out of the United States service, by Colonel Loomis, of the 5th United States Infantry. In the afternoon a final parade was made by the entire regiment, but F Company were obliged to leave the line before its conclusion, in order to take the 5 P. M. boat for home.

A few days after the arrival home of the company, a beautiful set of flags was received by Mayor Cranston, a gift from Rhode Islanders residing in California to the color company of the 1st Rhode Island Regiment, and were accompanied by the following explanatory letter:

San Francisco, Cal., Aug. 30, 1861.

Hon. WM. H. CRANSTON, Mayor City Newport:—

Sir,—At a meeting of the natives and citizens of Rhode Island now residents of California, we, the undersigned, were appointed a committee to forward to your Honor a set of regimental colors for the First Rhode Island Regiment, to be by you presented to them in person as a token of our esteem and admiration for the prompt, noble and efficient response made by them to the patriotic call of our country to fight for constitutional liberty, and for the brave, honorable and veteran-like manner in which they have performed their duties.

Very Respectfully, your obedient servants,
    WILLIAM SHERMAN,
    E. P. PECKHAM,
    JAS. M. OLNEY,
    B. H. RANDOLPH,
    C. V. S. GIBBS.

On Tuesday, October 29th, 1861, a formal presentation of the flags to Company F took place on Touro Park. The company were present in good numbers, and Colonel Burnside was also present by invitation. Mayor Cranston, after reading the correspondence accompanying the flags, remarked as follows:

"Company F, accept this offering—our unconquered and unconquerable national flag—and this State standard, the emblem of freedom for more than two hundred years—the patriotic and cheerful gift of Rhode Islanders in the Eden of the Pacific to you, their brothers in the Eden of the Atlantic. Guard them sacredly and well—carefully preserve and affectionately cherish them; if necessary, lay down your lives in their defence against foreign invasion or domestic insurrection, and your reward will be the gratitude of honest and loyal men on earth, the approbation of God, and eternal felicity in that new Paradise where there will neither be wars nor rumors of wars, and where the King of Kings and the Prince of Peace will reign supreme forever."

Colonel Burnside responded. After a few remarks acknowledging the kindness of the patriotic Californians, he turned to the members of Company F and addressed them as follows:

"With you, Company F, I leave these colors. For their proper keeping I need give you no charge. You have been tried and have indeed been found not wanting. Take them; accept them as a part of the history of the First Rhode Island Regiment, as a part of the history of your own gallant state and as an emblem of the glory of your dearly loved country. Love the one flag and revere the others. Many dark hours we have already passed through, and many more are yet to be undergone. But let no man of us falter as to the success of our glorious cause. In all our work, however dangerous or arduous, we shall be followed by the prayers of loved friends at home and of the true and loyal of all our country, and of the good and true of every land. The great God above may chasten us in his wisdom, but rest assured He will never forsake us in His justice. To you, Mr. Mayor, I render my sincere thanks for your kind words of me. They are indeed precious to me. The words of commendation which have been spoken of my conduct by my approving fellow citizens are my highest reward. And as to Company F, I have no fears but they will do as they have done before—their whole duty. Better soldiers never trod the soil of this or any other land. Not a man of them failed to execute my orders to the letter. Never soldiers did their duty—their whole duty—more promptly or gallantly. Take these beautiful flags, Company F, take them and keep them; you have the well earned right to keep them. Twice was your own flag stricken down in the field of battle and then a third man from your ranks seized it and it was borne aloft in safety from the field though pierced with many bullets.

Then turning to the Mayor, he added:

"And in conclusion allow me to thank you, sir, and all concerned in this presentation, for this beautiful gift to Rhode Island's first and gallant regiment."

Company F then made a parade through the city, displaying the flags.

At a meeting held by Company F at the armory of the Artillery Company, November 5th, 1861, it was voted to place the flags in charge of three members of Company F, and Corporal Tayer and Privates DeBlois and Terrell were appointed that committee, with instructions to place them in the Newport city hall for safe keeping. It was soon afterwards ascertained that the place allotted to them in the city hall was damp, and it was decided to remove them to a place where they would be better preserved, and could be seen at any time. The place selected was the Artillery Company's armory, where they were suitably mounted, and will doubtless always remain.

Soon after the muster out of F Company, recruiting commenced at once for new regiments from Rhode Island, and of 108 officers and men composing Company F at muster out, 84 re-entered the service either in the army or navy, many of them occupying positions of rank in both branches of the service during the war.

CONCLUSION

Company F, 1st Rhode Island Regiment, is a thing of the past. Thirty years have come and gone since the enactment of the stirring scenes in which we participated; but those scenes and incidents still exist in the minds and memories of the men composing that company. A large portion of its members have left the city, and many have been carried to that silent camp where they "sleep their last sleep, have fought their last battle; no sound can awake them to glory again." But as each succeeding 17th of April rolls around, the surviving members of the company meet to talk over the incidents of the long ago, tell stories of camp and field, and say a word of those who have left us to return no more; and we shall continue these gatherings at least once a year, until the last man of Company F shall have been mustered out to join those who have gone before.

www.ingramcontent.com/pod-product-compliance
Lightning Source LLC
Chambersburg PA
CBHW032137090426
42743CB00007B/623